YOUR KNOWLEDGE HAS VALUE

Aleks Ancenko

Death Penalty. A Comparison Between Germany and American Attitudes Towards Capital Punishment

GRIN Publishing

Bibliographic information published by the German National Library:

The German National Library lists this publication in the National Bibliography;
detailed bibliographic data are available on the Internet at http://dnb.dnb.de .

Imprint:

Copyright © 2012 GRIN Verlag GmbH
Print and binding: Books on Demand GmbH, Norderstedt Germany
ISBN: 978-3-656-94942-8

This book at GRIN:

http://www.grin.com/en/e-book/298393/death-penalty-a-comparison-between-
germany-and-american-attitudes-towards

GRIN - Your knowledge has value

Since its foundation in 1998, GRIN has specialized in publishing academic texts by students, college teachers and other academics as e-book and printed book. The website www.grin.com is an ideal platform for presenting term papers, final papers, scientific essays, dissertations and specialist books.

Visit us on the internet:

http://www.grin.com/

http://www.facebook.com/grincom

http://www.twitter.com/grin_com

BELEGARBEIT

im Fach Englisch

Death penalty – a comparison between German and American attitudes towards capital punishment

Dresden, 23.12.2012

Table of Contents

1 Introduction

October, 10th is known for being the "International Day Against the Death Penalty". It was also the day the author of the term paper watched the movie 'Green Line', in which an innocent black man was sentenced to death. It made her think about this kind of punishment and if it really is the right way to have somebody serving a sentence. She also realized that some countries still exercise the capital punishment, especially the USA. And she was also wondering how could two democracies, like Germany and the United States could have developed in such opposite directions.

In the following term paper the author is going to compare the German and American attitude toward the death penalty. At first she wants to clarify the definition. This paper will give a brief overview of the recent history of capital punishment in both states. The emphasis is on the comparison between these different attitudes. Providing to the findings of the German attitude the author indents to carry out a survey. Finally, she would like to express her own opinion on the topic.

2   Definition of the death penalty

Death as punishment was originally known as vendetta in ancient. It was allowed to take revenge on the murderer of your relatives. Today the death penalty is the most controversial punishment world-wide. By definition it is a provided for by statute homicide as a sentence for a capital crime. In the ordinary criminal law the death penalty is usually imposed for murder. Some states also punish other direct and indirect crimes against life and health of persons with death:

- Trafficking (China)
- Robbery resulting in death (United States)
- Bank Robbery (Saudi Arabia)
- Abduction
- Drug trafficking and possession of drugs above a certain amount
  (Indonesia, Saudi Arabia, Malaysia, Singapore, Thailand, Taiwan)
- Rape (China, Saudi Arabia)
- terrorist attacks on oil and gas pipelines (India)

The act has been banned in many countries. There are over 140 countries, which have abolished this kind of punishment. 58 states continue the enforcement. The majority of executions which have taken place in year 2010 were in China, Iran, North Korea, Yemen and the United States. These states have an age requirement to fulfil the homicide, but there is also a possibility to levy a death penalty on a minor (only in certain cases).

The standard method of execution is the lethal injection. Other ways of execution are shooting, the gas chamber, hanging and the electric chair. The four most practiced execution methods in 2011 were:

- Lethal injection in China, Taiwan and USA
- Beheading in Saudi Arabia
- Hanging in Egypt, Afghanistan, Bangladesh, Iraq, North Korea and South Sudan
- Shooting in Belarus, China, Yemen, North Korea, Palestinian Territories and
  Somalia [1]

3 Historical aspects of the death penalty

For thousands of years very serious crimes were penalized by death. In pre- state societies an unwritten family law allowed the relatives of a murder victim to take revenge with the offender and his family. With an increasing sedentariness rules and obligations become necessary. The first known law with a death penalty arose around 1700 BC.

3.1 History of the death penalty in Germany

The death penalty has a long history in Germany. At the time of the Empire the legal position of the death penalty was inconsistent. Since 1871 the death penalty was imposed for murder and attempted murder of the emperor or ruler. The executions during the Weimar Republic dropped steadily, but an application of the SPD in 1927 to abolish the law was rejected.

Immediately after the seizure of power by the Nazis in March 1933 they issued the "kingdom act and imposition of the death penalty". The crimes expanded so it was imposed for any offense from 1944 under "healthy popular sentiment". Between 1933 and 1945, 16560 death sentences were imposed, approximately 12,000 of them were enforced. After the failed assassination on Hitler especially many executions and mass executions were made.

3.1.1 GDR
The Soviet occupation force was responsible for hundreds of killings in the 1940s and 1950s. In the GDR the death penalty was inflicted for murder, espionage, war crimes, sabotage and counter-revolutionary crimes'. Death sentences were announced in show trials, the executions took place under strict secrecy. The truth revealed after the turnaround. The GDR abolished the death penalty officially in 1987.

3.1.2 FRG
During the Nuremberg Trials there were a majority of executions because of war crimes and crimes against humanity. Federal death sentences were carried out until 1951 in prisons in the U.S. Army on German soil. Until the founding of the Federal Republic of Germany in 1949 the application within the countries was inconsistent. The constitution declared the death penalty to be abolished.

Although when the penal laws still contain appropriate provisions, they could no longer be enforced, and were formally replaced by life imprisonment. According to the German Basic Law and privacy laws the abolition of the death penalty is absolute and unchangeable, and is to carry into all future German constitutions. It is a non-tenable fundamental right that can't be rescinded by any legislative initiative. [2]

3.2 History of the death penalty in the USA

In the United States, the history of the death penalty dates back to the beginning of the 17th Century at the time of colonial settlement, the British colonial rulers brought this aspect of penalties from their old homeland, where executions were carried out for centuries, and also used for small offenses. 1608, the British Captain George Kendall in Virginia was executed for spying for Spain, he became the first victim of the death penalty. Later, especially in the 18th Century there were first considerations and efforts to abolish the death penalty in America. Even Thomas Jefferson was planning a change in Virginia's criminal laws so that only treason and murder should be punished with death, but it failed in Parliament. 1794 Pennsylvania abolished the death penalty for all crimes except murder (including first degree murder). Subsequently many other states reduced the number of possible crimes which were punished with the death. In the 19th Century more and more people wanted to abolish the death penalty. Pennsylvania led the way, when they stopped do the executions in public and remove them to a place where only selected witnesses where allowed to watch. In 1846 Michigan punished only treason by death. Rhode Iceland and Wisconsin abolished the law completely. In the south states changed almost nothing. During the American Civil War in the 1860s the support for the abolition of the death penalty in the United States declined. The focus was almost entirely on the abolition of slavery. Then the sentence was modernized with the introduction of the electric chair (invented by Thomas Edison). Nevertheless the resistance against the death penalty grew. Between 1907 and 1917 a complete abolition took place in six states. This reform was short-lived, 1920 had five of the six countries already introduced the death penalty again. 1924 first came to the gas chamber used. During the years from 1920 to 1940 the death penalty was more supported again. This was due to the developments in Europe, but also due to the depression and prohibition. In the 30s, there were more executions than any other time. Annual average of 167 people was executed.

After the Second World War and after the United Nations had declared the right to live in their Declaration of Human Rights in 1948, the death penalty was impose in the U.S. much less. Many other nations abolished the death penalty completely. The number of supporters declined also in America. This reflects the change in public attitudes on the issue. It was also expressed in the fact that the U.S Supreme Court dealt with the question of the legality of the death penalty. This legal uncertainty declined the execution in the United States in 1968. In June 1972 the Supreme Court made the decision to interdict the death penalty in 40 states. The reason was that the consummation of the death sentences was unconstitutional. In 1976 the Supreme Court re-examined the new law and confirmed. In Utah was the first death sentence carried out since 1968 in January 1977. In 1986 the Supreme Court has forbidden the executions of mentally ill persons. Till 2011 New Jersey, New Mexico and Illinois abolished the death penalty. [3], [5]

4 Attitudes towards the death penalty

4.1 Attitudes of the German citizens towards the death penalty

The current Constitution of Germany prohibits the death penalty. This law came into effect in 1949 and is stated in article 102. With the founding of the Federal Republic the capital punishment has been abolished in the western part of Germany. But in 1949, 55 % of the population were in favour of the death penalty. The political orientation has remained a stable predictor towards the attitudes. The Left- wing parties always supported the abolition of the capital punishment. The SPD had made several attempts in the "Weimar Republic" and always failed due to votes of the Conservatives. The strongest supporters of the capital punishment are voters of the DVU and PDS (both parties no longer exist), most opponents are to be found within the ranks of the Green Party and the FDP. 54 % of the CDU -followers also admitted to be in favour of an execution for serious crimes. About 90 % of the Greens strongly oppose the death penalty.

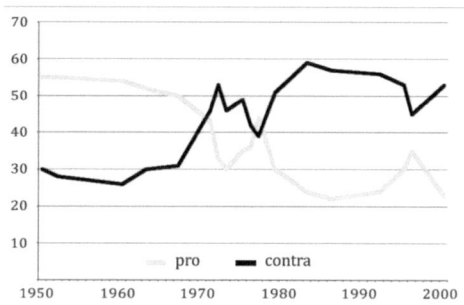

The death penalty in the Federal Republic of setting 1950-2000 (Photo credit: © Historeo 2012)

The following line graph shows the development of the attitude of German citizens towards the death penalty from 1950 till 2000. In 1952 the Allensbach Institute found out that 55 % of the Germans were basically in favour of the death penalty, only 28% opposed it. The statistics show a sudden change in the 70ies. The number of people who oppose the capital punishment has increased since 1978, while the number of supporters has decreased. When comparing the numbers in 2000 one can state clearly that there are fewer supporters than opponents. The statistics show that the number of defenders has halved in 2000.

The development of the attitude towards the capital punishment in Germany shows that abolition can find a later legitimization even when at first the majority of the people opposed it. In 1949, the majority's opinion was that a constitutional state should not renounce this extreme sort of punishment. The solidly developing judicial system led to dramatic change in public opinions. The courageous first step of the constitutional giver can influence the public opinion and so it did. [2]

4.2   The attitude of Americans towards the death penalty

The best known fact about American attitude toward the death penalty is the support. Even when the number of people executed each year has fallen. Between 1992 and 2003, the number of criminal serving a life sentence increased by 83%. Studies have shown that Westerners favoured the death penalty the most, while Midwesterners and Easterners favoured it the least.The political orientation has remained a stable predictor the attitudes. 85% the defenders were Republicans and 61% Democrats, as were 78% of conservatives and 62% of liberals.

The following statistics shows the public opinion on the death penalty from 1936 till 1994. The support of the death penalty is long term solidly and growing. Knowledge about miscarriages of justice which can be numerously booked with the help of DNA test initiated a change. The support for the death penalty declined to a low of 47 % in 1996. On the other hand the opponent was on its high with 50 %. When comparing the percentages in 1994 one can state clearly that they are five times as much defenders as opposers. This high level of support might be explained as a reaction to the sharp increase in homicide and other violent crimes.

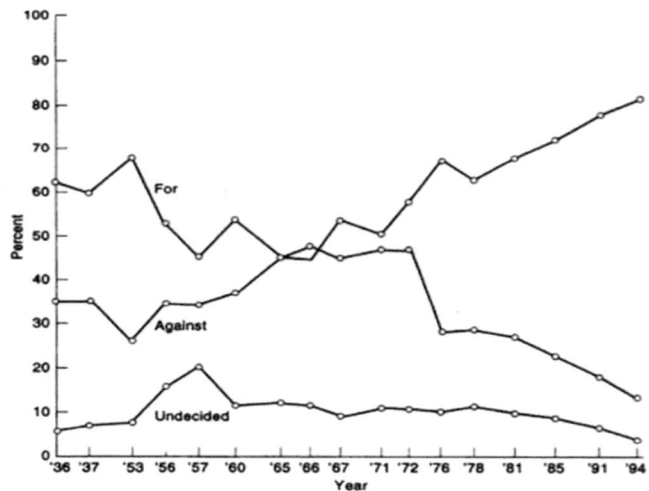

Hugo Adam Bedau: The Death Penalty in America. New York: Oxford University Press 1997, S.105

The second statistics shows the attitude toward the capital punishment by gender and race from 1952 toll 1992. The line graph shows a slow increase of defenders from 1952 to 1966. It illustrates also a slow growth of supporters from 1966. By comparing the numbers we might come to the conclusion that man and Whites are more likely to support the death penalty than woman and Blacks.[3] [5]

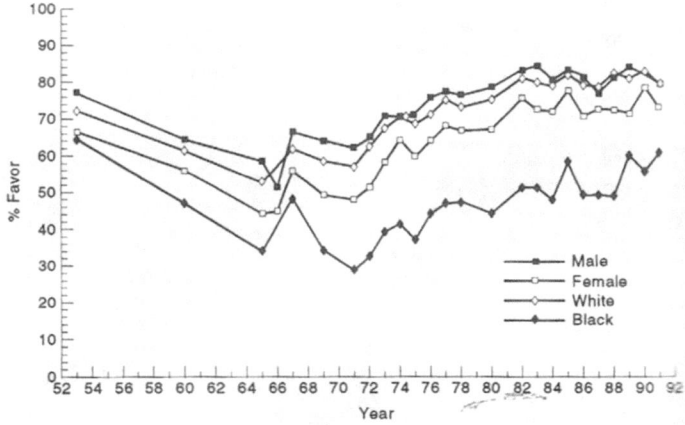

Hugo Adam Bedau: The Death Penalty in America. New York: Oxford University Press 1997, S.924.

4.3 Comparison of the American and German viewpoint

The capital punishment is abolished in most democracies. The USA is not that far yet. In a comparison between German and US-American development the differences outweigh. As the statistics show the attitude in the United States is the exact opposite to Germany. The opinion there might correspond with Germany's attitude before the abolition. In 2000, 70 % of Americans supported the death penalty and 28 % opposed it. Remarkable is the similarity to Germany in 1948, when 70% were in favour and 20% appose. The support of the capital punishment in the US is long term solidly and growing. The support had its high in 1988.

The line graph of Germans views show a completely change in peoples mind since 1948. The numbers show a steady increase of defenders and a decrease of supporters.

The capital punishment has been abolished in Germany despite majority support. The development of the attitude toward the capital punishment in Germany shows that an abolition by the constitution can find a later legitimisation. The legal position of the capital punishment in the United States depends on popular support. There is no chance to abolition the death penalty while the population support it like it was in Germany.[4]

Source: own research

Source: own research

5   Own opinion

Germany does not longer have the death penalty. The last criminal to be executed was in the 1981 by hanging. The detailed discussion about the death penalty encouraged the author in her opinion. The author is opposed to the death penalty. She does not think that death is a 'punishment' at all. It is more a release than a punishment. Everyone who is sentenced to death has no chance to think about what they have done and to repent. They escape a real punishment, where they have to live with what they have done to others. In the authors opinion a life imprisonment is more severe as a punishment. Another point to consider is that an execution cost more than a life in prison.

Moreover, the writer thinks that it is not fair to kill a human being, even if they killed someone. It is not right to take someone others life, no matter what. The capital punishment is inhuman and person-despising. She thinks the danger to execute an innocent person is too big. There are numerous cases in which it has eventually turned out that the executed "criminal" was not guilty of the crime he was charged with at all. If an innocent person is sentenced to death it can't be cancelled. But if he is sentenced to a life imprisonment his innocence can be proved and he will be free.

11

The capital punishment makes the world not a better and safer place. The execution of the culprits does not bring back to life the victims again. The writer feels like the death penalty is just as wrong as the original crime committed. All in all she does not believe that the killing of another human being can be justified by a reference to the wrongs committed by the victim.

6   Survey

Question: What is your view on the death penalty?
Possible answers: in favour; in favour (just in certain cases); oppose; no opinion

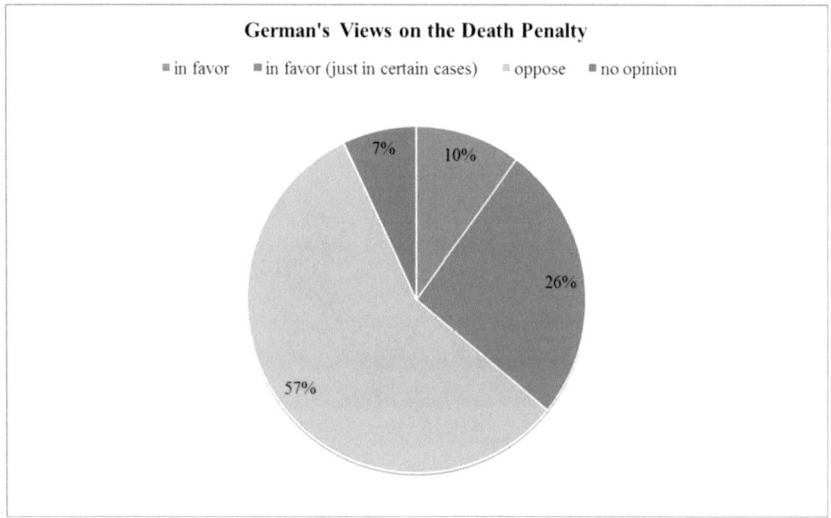

Source: own research

The pie chart relates to a poll from 2012. 100 people were interviewed in the age 16-25. First of all the writer would like to mention that there is given the attitudes of young people toward the death penalty. When comparing the percentages one can state clearly that they are less supporters. 36 % are in favour of the death penalty, while 57 % oppose. 7 % had no opinion. More surprising was the fact that more women were in favour of the capital punishment than men. When comparing the differences between the genders in other polls the result was quite the opposite. Apart from that the small poll is representative for the German attitude if you compare the results to bigger polls.

7 Bibliography

Sources:

[1]   Death Penalty Law Law & Legal Definition- In: http://definitions.uslegal.com/d/death-penalty-law/ (Abruf vom 27.12.2012)

Amnesty International Schweiz :Todesstrafe Zahlen und Fakten. –
In: http://www.amnesty.ch/de/themen/todesstrafe/facts-figures (Abruf vom 27.12.2012)

ALIVE - Koalition gegen die Todesstrafe e.V.Ä: Exekutionsmethoden.
In: http://www.todesstrafe-usa.de/de/info/methoden.html (Abruf vom 27.12.2012)

[2]   ALIVE - Koalition gegen die Todesstrafe e.V.: Ein Blick in die Geschichte –
In: http://www.todesstrafe-usa.de/de/info/geschichte.html (Abruf vom 28.12.2012)

Wikimedia Foundation Inc.: Todesstrafe –
In: http://de.wikipedia.org/wiki/Todesstrafe#1800_bis_1945 (Abruf vom 28.12.2012)

Michael Kahr: Die Geschichte der Todesstrafe in der ehemaligen DDR Teil-1. –
In:http://www.todesstrafe.de/artikel/78/Die_Geschichte_der_Todesstrafe_in_der_ehemaligen_DDR_Teil-1.html (Abruf vom 28.12.2012)

Geschichte der Todesstrafe: Amnesty International Schweiz. – In:
http://www.amnesty.ch/de/themen/todesstrafe/info/geschichte-der-todesstrafe
(Abruf vom 27.12.2012)

[3]   Lars Hoffmann: Geschichte der Todesstrafe in den USA. –
In: http://www.americanet.de/html/todesstrafe__geschichte.html (Abruf vom 29.12.2012)

Wikimedia Foundation Inc.: Todesstrafe in den Vereinigten Staaten. –
In: http://de.wikipedia.org/wiki/Todesstrafe_in_den_Vereinigten_Staaten   (Abruf   vom
28.12.2012)

ALIVE - Koalition gegen die Todesstrafe e.V : Geschichte USA. – In:
http://www.todesstrafe-usa.de/de/info/geschichte_usa.html (Abruf vom 28.12.2012)

David Masci: An Impassioned Debate: An Overview of the Death Penalty in America. – In:
http://www.pewforum.org/Death-Penalty/An-Impassioned-Debate-An-Overview-of-the-Death-Penalty-in-America.aspx (Abruf vom 5.02.2013)

David Masci: Public Opinion on the Death Penalty. – In:
http://www.pewforum.org/Death-Penalty/Public-Opinion-on-the-Death-Penalty.aspx (Abruf vom 8.02.2013)

Death Penalty Information Center: Public Opinion About the Death Penalty. – In:
http://www.deathpenaltyinfo.org/public-opinion-about-death-penalty
(Abruf vom 8.02.2013)

Martin Haidinger: Todesstrafe. In: http://www.americanet.de/todesstrafe.html
(Abruf vom 9.02.2013)

Sueddeutsche: Demokraten für die Todesstrafe. In:
http://www.sueddeutsche.de/politik/todesstrafe-in-den-usa-der-staat-als-raecher-1.5029-3
(Abruf vom 12.02.2013)

[4]   Christoph Drösser: Keine Scharfrichter. – In: http://www.zeit.de/2008/12/Stimmts-Todes-
strafe (Abruf vom 12.02.2013)

Ipsos-Public Affairs / Associated Press: Death Penalty Backed in Four Countries. – In:
http://www.angus-reid.com/polls/3045/death_penalty_backed_in_four_countries/
(Abruf vom 13.02.2013)

Mirko Gründe: 1952: Keine Wiedereinführung der Todesstrafe in Deutschland. – In:
http://www.historeo.de/datum/todesstrafe-in-deutschland-debatte-1952
(Abruf vom 12.02.2013)

Prof. Dr. Arthur Kreuzer: Die Abschaffung der Todesstrafe in Deutschland – mit Verglei-
chen zur Entwicklung. – In: http://www.zis-online.com/dat/artikel/2006_8_50.pdf.
(Abruf vom 7.02.2013)

Literature:

[5]   Hugo Adam Bedau: The Death Penalty in America. New York: Oxford University Press
1997

Laura E. Randa: Society's Final Solution. Maryland: University Press of America 1997